MW01110264

Queen Helen's
Bug Buddies

Irene T. Hunt, Author and Photographer
Timothy J. Hunt, Editor and Photographer

Hunt for Nature Publishing
San Diego, California

www.HuntForNature.com

Special thanks to

Tim Hunt...my best buddy and pal for life!

Mark and Priscilla Whitbeck...the most creative and inspiring playmates ever!

Carly, Kate and Wesley Hunt...the best 9 and 7 year old teachers I've ever had!

My family and friends for their love, encouragement and support!

Rod and Robin Deutschmann for imparting their knowledge of, and passion for, photography!

Jim Nelson for asking all the right questions and expecting answers!

Susan Walker for sharing her valuable knowledge and insights!

Tanya Clayton for her incredible patience and software mastery!

Nate Robb for his amazing illustrations!

San Diego Botanic Garden (formerly Quail Botanical Gardens) and the beautiful great outdoors, both of which are home to all of Queen Iween's bug buddies.

***

Roly-Poly and Praying Mantis photographs courtesy of Mark and Priscilla Whitbeck

***

Copyright © 2009 by Irene T. Hunt
All rights reserved. Except as permitted under the U.S. Copyright Act of 1796, no part of this publication may be reproduced, distributed or transmitted in any form or by any means, or stored in a database or retrieval system, without the prior written permission of the publisher.

Library of Congress Control Number: 2009911369
Summary: Queen Iween entertains and educates children on her bug buddies and friends.
ISBN #978-0-9843071-0-4
[1. Children 2. Bugs 3. Insects 4. Photography 5. Nature]
First Edition: November 2009   10 9 8 7 6 5 4 3 2 1

Hunt for Nature Publishing
San Diego, California

For information about Hunt for Nature Publishing visit our website at www.HuntForNature.com
or send an email to QueenIween@HuntForNature.com.

Hi!
My name is Queen Iween.
What's your name?

My friends and I are so happy to
meet you. Do you have friends?

My friends are probably a lot like your
friends. We all look different and act
differently. Each of us is special
in our own way.

I have tall friends, short friends,
creepy friends, crawly friends, shy
friends, and friends that like
to sing and dance.

Are you ready to
meet them?

My friends are excited to meet you!

Their names and page numbers are...

This is my friend, Spike.
He is a Fly.

Flies are very fast! Spike's wings beat more than
200 times a second. That is fast!

Spike is a very hairy fly. His hair helps him to feel things and taste things. When there is movement close to Spike his hairs can feel it, even before he can see it. That is why flies are so hard to catch. Spike's hair also works like a tongue. When he lands on something his hairs tell him if it is good to eat or not.

Flies are always in search of food so they will land on anything and everything. That makes him a very dirty guy, my friend Spike the Fly.

Spike the Fly

Flies are faster than any of my other bug buddies! Their wings beat more than 200 times a second.

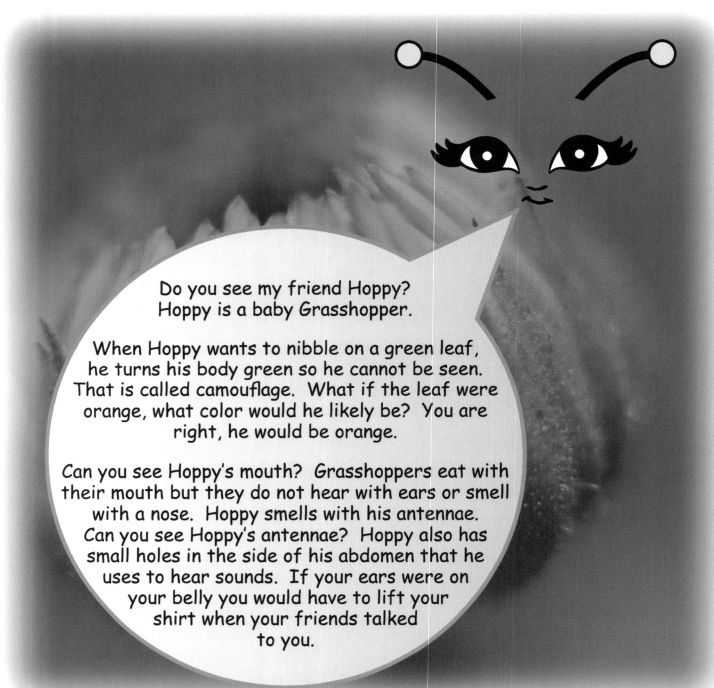

Do you see my friend Hoppy?
Hoppy is a baby Grasshopper.

When Hoppy wants to nibble on a green leaf,
he turns his body green so he cannot be seen.
That is called camouflage. What if the leaf were
orange, what color would he likely be? You are
right, he would be orange.

Can you see Hoppy's mouth? Grasshoppers eat with
their mouth but they do not hear with ears or smell
with a nose. Hoppy smells with his antennae.
Can you see Hoppy's antennae? Hoppy also has
small holes in the side of his abdomen that he
uses to hear sounds. If your ears were on
your belly you would have to lift your
shirt when your friends talked
to you.

Hoppy the Grasshopper

Grasshoppers can smell
with their antennae
and hear through small
holes in their abdomen.

Who does this look like? You are right, she looks like me.

I am a Honey Bee and so is Hannah. We are family. Do you look like your mother, father, brother, or sister?

Hannah is collecting pollen in her pollen baskets so she can carry it back to the hive. Can you see the pollen basket on Hannah's back leg?

Did you know that some types of Honey Bees dance? It is their way of communicating with each other. Their dance movements are signals to the other bees in the hive.

Can you do a Honey Bee dance with me?

Hannah the Honey Bee

Honey Bees pollinate flowers, plants, and crops as they collect food for the hive.

Meet my friend Sammy.
Sammy is a Snail.

He is a slippery, two-eyed,
one-footed, slimy dude. He just
loves his slime because it keeps
him moist and helps him glide.
Snails have one, and only one, foot.

Can you find Sammy's foot? No?
Well, Sammy's foot is the part of his
body that he crawls on. He uses his
foot to glide from place to place and
to feel things. Sammy's eyesight
is not very good so he has to
use his sense of smell and
touch to find his food.

Sammy the Snail

Did you know that snails can crawl upside down without falling?
The slime on their foot gives them the ability to hold on to things.

Ryan the Roly-Poly Bug is one of my best buddies.

Roly-Poly Bugs do not like daylight so they come out at night, this is called nocturnal. Ryan is nocturnal just like many of my other bug buddies.

Did you know that Roly-Poly Bugs can curl up in a ball? Do you know why they do that? It is how they protect themselves.

It must be fun to be able to turn into a ball whenever you want. Can you curl up in a ball?

Ryan the Roly-Poly Bug

Roly-Poly Bugs
curl up in a ball to
protect themselves.

This is Dizzy
the Dragonfly.

I call him Dizzy because I get
dizzy when I watch him fly.
He can hover, do loop-the-loops,
and fly backward.

Dizzy has two sets of wings. Each
set of wings can flap in a different
direction. Dizzy's wings can flap
30 beats per second.

Is Dizzy faster than Spike the
fly who can beat his wings more
than 200 times per second?
No, Spike is much faster,
but Spike cannot fly
backward like Dizzy.

Dizzy the Dragonfly

Dragonflies have two big eyes that are close together.
It looks like they are wearing a helmet, like jet pilots.

This is Stinky!

I call him Stinky because he is a Stink Beetle. Would you like to be named Stinky?

Stinky does not play well with people. I think they scare him so he likes to come out at night when everyone is sleeping. Can you remember what that is called? Nocturnal is right.

If you scare Stinky he will do a handstand. He will put his head on the ground and raise his bottom in the air. Then watch out! He will try to squirt you with a stinky black liquid.

I would not scare Stinky if I were you, or you will be stinky too!

18

Stinky the Stink Beetle

When a Stink Beetle has his head on the ground
and his bottom in the air he is getting ready to squirt you!

This is my friend Lady the Ladybug.

Can you see the spots on Lady's wings? No? That is because she does not have any spots. Some Ladybugs have spots, some do not, and some even lose their spots as they get older.

Ladybugs cannot fly when the weather gets cold, instead they have to crawl. When they do fly they can beat their wings up to 85 times per second.

Who do you think can fly faster, Lady the Ladybug or Spike the Fly, who beats his wings 200 times a second?

Lady the Ladybug

Ladybugs help protect plants by eating bugs that hurt plants.

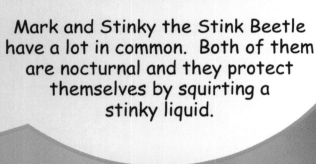

Look at all those little legs
on my friend Mark the Millipede!

Mark has two pairs of legs for each
segment (part) of his body. Mark's body
grows longer each time he sheds; the more he
sheds the more legs he grows. With so many
legs it is hard for Mark to move fast. If he
does he will trip. Do you ever trip
over your own two feet?

Mark and Stinky the Stink Beetle
have a lot in common. Both of them
are nocturnal and they protect
themselves by squirting a
stinky liquid.

Mark the Millipede

When a Millipede's body grows longer it grows more legs.

Say "Hi" to my friend Dara.
She is a Damselfly. Damselflies are
smaller than dragonflies. They also have
different eyes and wings.

Dara has two big round eyes, one on each side of
her head. Can you see Dara's eyes? Dara is different
than Dizzy the Dragonfly. Dizzy has eyes that are close
together and cover most of his head. Dizzy looks like
he is wearing a helmet, like a jet pilot.

When Dara is resting she holds her wings along the
side of her body. Dragonflies have larger wings
that they hold out from their body, like
the wings of an airplane.

Dara the Damselfly

Damselflies have two big round eyes,
one on each side of their head.
Dragonflies have eyes that are close
together and cover most of their head.

Here is my friend Priscilla
the Praying Mantis.

Priscilla has more eyes than you.
She has two large eyes with three smaller
eyes between them. How many eyes does
she have? With five eyes Priscilla can see
very far. She can see movement as far away
as 60 feet.

Praying Mantises also have ultrasonic hearing
and quick arms. With their great eyesight,
hearing, and fast arms they can catch
their food easily. Priscilla can also
camouflage herself like Hoppy the
Grasshopper. She has many
special talents.

Priscilla the Praying Mantis

Praying Mantises have ultrasonic hearing, just like bats.

Skip is my Butterfly buddy.
He is a Fiery Skipper Butterfly.

Skip drinks flower juice called nectar.
He has a very long tongue-like straw
that he keeps curled up under his chin.

When Skip is thirsty he uncurls his straw
and uses it to suck the nectar
from flowers. His straw works just
like the straw you use to drink
your juice.

Skip the Butterfly

Butterflies help to pollinate plants as they move from flower to flower, just like honey bees.

Say hello to my friend Wes!

Wes is a Paper Wasp. He is called a Paper Wasp because his nest is made of wood fibers and spit, which dries to look like paper.

It is not polite to spit unless you are Wes and you need to build your home.

Wes the Paper Wasp

Wasps living together are called a "colony."

My friend Archer is a Black Carpenter Ant.

He is small but very strong. Archer is so strong that he can carry more than three of his friends on his back at one time.

I bet you are pretty strong too, but your body is not built like Archer's body. He has three main body parts: a head, a thorax and an abdomen. He also has six legs, four more legs than you have, which gives him more strength.

Please do not put three friends on your back or you might get hurt.

Archer the Carpenter Ant

Carpenter Ants chew on dead wood
turning it into soil. Soil helps plants grow.

Say hello to my friend Shelby. He is a Shield Bug.

Shelby has four wings that cannot be seen because they are under his hard shell-like back. Shelby's back is a shield that protects his body, like the shields the knights used to protect their bodies.

Shield Bugs have another way of protecting themselves. Do you know what that might be? I will give you a hint: Mark the Millipede and Stinky the Stink Beetle have the same ability. You are right! Shelby can also squirt you with a smelly liquid.

Shelby the Shield Bug

Shield Bugs have hard shell-like backs that protect them. Their backs work just like a knight's shield.

My friend Kate is a baby Katydid.

Kate sure is pretty. She can change her colors whenever she feels like it, just like Hoppy the Grasshopper. Do you remember what that is called? You are right, it is called camouflage.

Katydids like the night more than the daylight. They are nocturnal just like my friends Stinky the Stink Beetle and Mark the Millipede.

Just before the sun goes down you might hear Katydids singing. Yes, Katydids can sing. Their song sounds like this, "Katy Did, Katy Didn't." Can you sing the Katydid song for me?

36

Kate the Katydid

As Katydids get older they grow wings that look
like leaves. This helps to camouflage them while they eat.

Carly the Monarch Caterpillar is very cool!

Carly has something in common with Spike the Fly, Stinky the Stink Beetle, Shelby the Shield Bug, Lady the Ladybug, Archer the Carpenter Ant, Hannah the Honey Bee, Skip the Butterfly, Wes the Paper Wasp and many other bugs. Do you know what that is?

They all have a four stage life cycle (egg, larva, pupa, and adult). This means that they change their physical form four times in their life. This is called a complete metamorphosis. One day Carly will turn into a beautiful Monarch Butterfly and I will take her picture for you.

Carly the Monarch Caterpillar

Monarch Caterpillars spend all
their time eating Milkweed plants,
which make them big and strong, so
they can turn into butterflies.

Now that you have met all my bug buddies what can you remember about them?

40

Queen Iween's Quiz

1. Which of my friends likes to sing?
   (Page 36)

2. Does Sammy the Snail have one foot, two feet, or three feet?
   (Page 12)

3. Why does Hannah the Honey Bee dance?
   (Page 10)

4. What does Wes the Paper Wasp build his house with?
   (Page 30)

5. Who has more legs, Mark the Millipede or Carly the Monarch Caterpillar?
   (Pages 23 and 39)

6. What are the names of my friends that can camouflage themselves?
   (Pages 8, 26, and 36)

7. Which of my friends can make you very smelly if you scare them?
   (Pages 18, 22 and 34)

8. Why does Ryan the Roly-Poly curl up into a ball?
   (Page 14)

9. Which one of my friends is the fastest?
   (Pages 6, 16 and 20)

10. Which one of my friends is your favorite bug buddy? Why?

_____, the Blue Dragonfly

ALL ABOUT ME

My name is _____.

I am _____ years old.

My favorite color is _____.

My favorite bug is a/an _____.

My favorite animal is a/an _____.

My favorite toy is a/an _____.

My favorite sport is _____.

ALL ABOUT MY FRIENDS

My friends' names are _____, _____ and _____.

Our favorite game to play is _____.

My friend, _____, is the funniest of all my friends.

We laugh a lot when _____.

We share the same interest in _____.

Thank you for visiting with me.
I hope you had fun learning about my
friends in nature. I feel very lucky to have
all types of friends. Even though they are
different, each of my friends is important to
me, and to the environment!

Well, I must fly home to my hive now, but
before I go I would like to remind you to
"Bee Nice and Bee Kind"
to all your friends and mine.

Glossary

Abdomen (ab-do-men)
  The part of the insect's body that is located behind the thorax.

Camouflage (cam-ou-flage)
  To blend into a background so as not to be seen.

Colony (col-o-ny)
  Several insects of the same family living together.

Metamorphosis (meta-mor-pho-sis)
  A change of physical form. A "complete metamorphosis" has four stages: egg, larva, pupa, and adult. An "incomplete metamorphosis" has three stages: egg, nymph (baby adult), and adult.

Nocturnal (noc-tur-nal)
  Active at night.

Pollinate (pol-li-nate)
  To transfer pollen from one plant or flower to another.

Thorax (tho-rax)
  The part of the insect's body that is located between the head and the abdomen.

Ultrasonic Hearing (ul-tra-son-ic)
  The ability to hear sounds that are above the range of human hearing.

LaVergne, TN USA
10 January 2010
169489LV00002B